What Did You See Out Your Windo

¿Qué viste hoy por tu ventana?

Leslie Handler

WHISTLESLICK PRESS

Publisher: Whistleslick Press

Publisher's Note: This is a work of fiction. Names, characters, places, and incidents are a product of the author's imagination. Locales and public names are sometimes used for atmospheric purposes. Any resemblance to actual people, living or dead, or to businesses, companies, events, institutions, or locales is completely coincidental.

Book design © 2017, BookDesignTemplates.com

Ordering Information: Special discounts are available on quantity purchases by corporations, associations, and others. For details, contact the author at the address above.

ISBN 978-1-949565-07-2

Printed in the United States of America

Acknowledgements & Dedications

A huge thank you to my parents and my children for always supporting, inspiring, encouraging and believing and to my nieces and nephews, of all ages, you know you fill my heart with joy.

Thank you to everyone who assisted with publication of this book, including Lori Perkins (Email: absolutepublishingservices@gmail.com) for all of her guidance from day one; P.J. HarteNaus for introducing me to Lori and giving me courage; Cat Hoogestraat (Email: amuttabove@gmail.com) for her delightful drawings of the signs; my sister, Cheryl Kelly (Email: cheryljkelly5161@yahoo.com), for simply asking "May I do the illustrations?"(I am so glad you did); and Jodie Toohey (Email: jodie@wordsywoman.com) for her editing and interior formatting.

A special thank you to Alexandra Saravia, a master of languages.

"Muchas Gracias" to Esther Uruchima for the translation of my poem and being there for me from the start!

A sincere note of thanks to the Editors at Modern Signs Press, developers of Signing Exact English, for granting permission to base the sign illustrations on their designs.

And finally, a huge thank you to my husband and best friend who has always made it so easy. I could not be me without you.

Lee Brett, Lee Brett, what did you see out your window today?

I saw 1 shimmering hummingbird in the brilliant blue sky out my window today.

brilliant   blue   sky

¿Lee Brett, Lee Brett, qué viste hoy por tu ventana?

Hoy ví un colibrí reluciente en el brillante cielo azul afuera de mi ventana.

Ryan, Ryan, what did you see out your window today?

I saw 2 grasshoppers out my window today.

One was basking in the sun.

One was leaping just for fun.

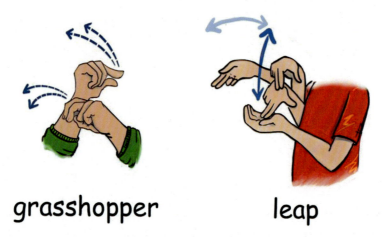

grasshopper   leap

¿Ryan, Ryan, qué viste hoy por tu ventana?

Hoy ví dos saltamontes afuera de mi ventana.

Uno estaba tomando el sol.

El otro estaba saltando sólo por diversión.

Bella, Bella, what did you see out your window today? I saw 3 squirrels out my window today. One was stretching upside down, reaching for the seeds before they fell to the ground. Two were running 'round and 'round.

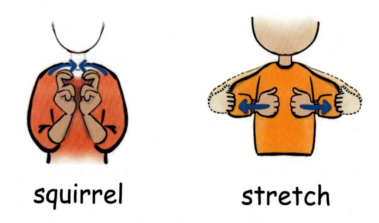

squirrel   stretch

¿Bella, Bella, qué viste hoy por tu ventana? Hoy ví tres ardillas afuera de mi ventana. Una estuvo estirandose boca abajo, alcanzando las semillas antes de que cayeran al suelo. Dos corrían dando vueltas y vueltas.

Dreiden, Dreiden, what did you see out your window today? I saw 4 woodpeckers out my window today. One I heard! One came flying through the air. One was picking the large nuts from the mix. One was performing its woodpecking tricks.

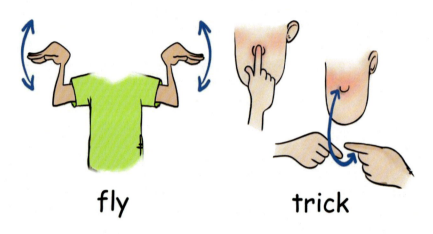

fly   trick

¿Dreiden, Dreiden, qué viste hoy por tu ventana? Hoy ví cuatro pájaros carpinteros afuera de mi ventana. ¡Yo escuché uno! Uno vino volando en el aire. Uno estuvo recogiendo las nueces grandes de la mezcla. Uno estuvo actuando los trucos de los pájaros carpinteros.

Lindsay, Lindsay, what did you see out your window today? I saw 5 turkeys out my window today. Five turkeys strolling past. The loudest gobbler was also the last.

turkey   loud   last

¿Lindsay, Lindsay, qué viste hoy por tu ventana? Hoy ví cinco pavos afuera de mi ventana. Cinco pavos paseando. El último fue el más bullicioso.

Stephen, Stephen, what did you see out your window today?

I saw 6 golden leaves out my window today.

Twirling, dancing leaves abound.

Performing ballet, without a sound.

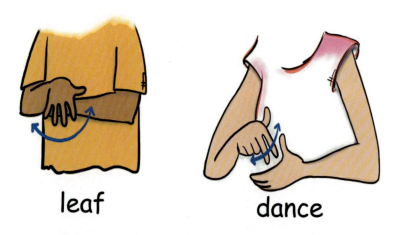

leaf   dance

¿Stephen, Stephen, qué viste hoy por tu ventana?

Hoy ví seis hojas doradas afuera de mi ventana.

Girando, bailando abundan las hojas.

Danzando un ballet sin sonido.

Katrina, Katrina, what did you see out your window today? I saw 7 butterflies out my window today. I tried to take photos of two, but getting too close, away they flew. Four more teased me with their beauty, so I could only snap one little cutie.

butterfly   beautiful   picture

¿Katrina, Katrina, qué viste hoy por tu ventana? Hoy ví siete mariposas afuera de mi ventana. Traté de tomar fotos a dos, pero cuando estaba muy cerca, ellas se fueron. Cuatro de ellas me ilusionaron por su belleza. Sólo pude ajustar una pequeña.

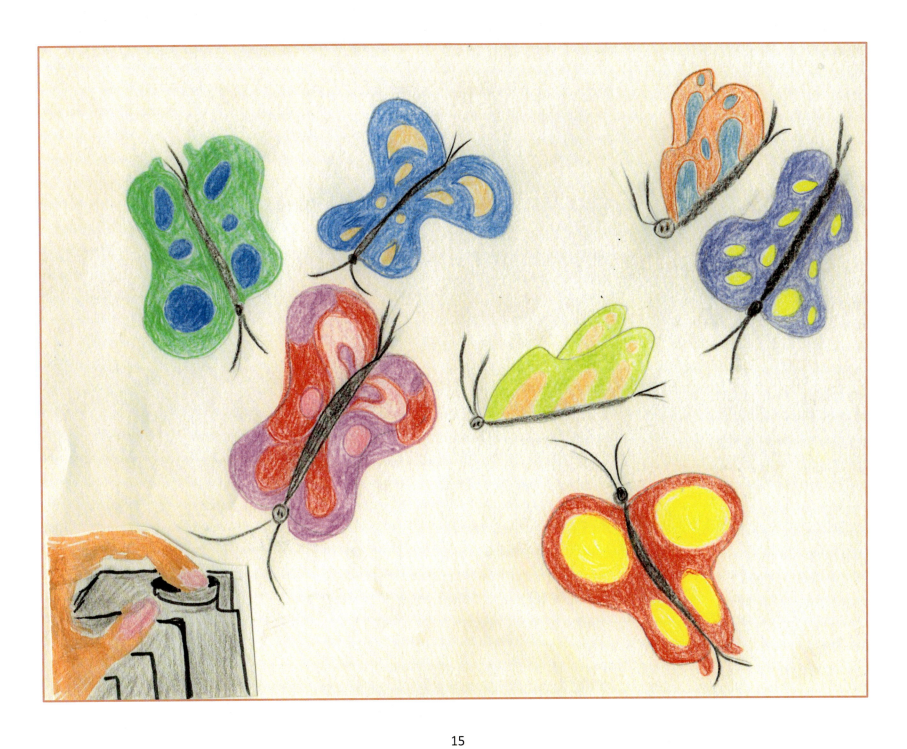

J.J., J.J., what did you see out your window today?

I saw 8 chipmunks out my window today.

Scampering, digging, hiding in holes.

They really were adorable souls.

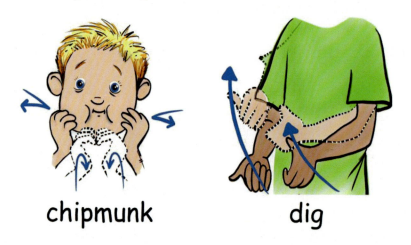

chipmunk   dig

¿J.J., J.J., qué viste hoy por tu ventana?

Hoy ví ocho ardillas afuera de mi ventana.

Correnteando, excavando y escodiendose en los agujeros.

Eran realmente unas almas adorables.

Rueben, Reuben, what did you see out your window today?

I saw 9 caterpillars out my window today.

They wiggled upon the grassy blade, making their way toward the cooling shade.

caterpillar   grass   wiggle

¿Reuben, Reuben, qué viste hoy por tu ventana?

Hoy ví nueve orugas afuera de mi ventana.

Ellas se meneaban sobre las hierbas,

haciendo su camino hasta las refrescantes sombras.

Lee Brett, Ryan, Bella, Dreiden, Lindsay, Stephen, Katrina, J.J., and Reuben, what did you all see out your window today? We all saw 10 trees out our window today. Ten trees to flower, ten trees to bloom. Ten trees to shade with plenty of room.

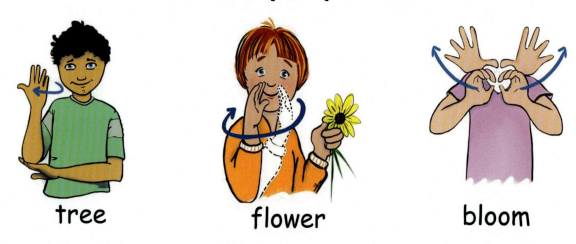

tree   flower   bloom

¿Lee Brett, Ryan, Bella, Dreiden, Lindsay, Stephen, Katrina, J.J., y Reuben, que víeron uds hoy por la ventana? Hoy nosotros vimos diez árboles. Diez árboles a flor, diez árboles a florecer. Diez árboles para sombra con amplio espacio.

THE ALPHABET

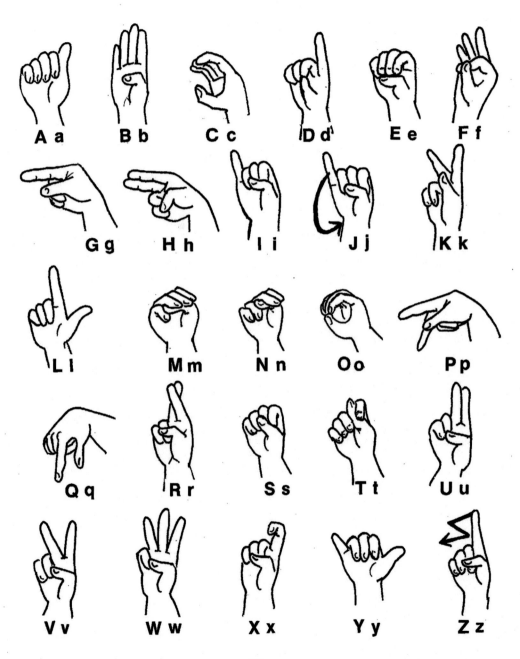

NUMBERS

One (1)

Two (2)

Three (3)

Four (4)

Five (5)

Six (6)

Seven (7)

Eight (8)

Nine (9)